Modal Jams & Theory
Using The Modes For Solo Guitar
by Dave Celentano
Foreword by Marty Friedman

Special thanks to: my wife Kris, the Celentano Family, the Leggitt family, Ron Middlebrook, Frank Green at D'Angelico strings, Grayson's Music, Gard's Music, Wayne Charvel, Eric Galletta and God for the special gift of music.

SAN 683-8022
ISBN 0-931759-76-5

Cover Art - Eddie Young
Music Notation - Derek Cornet
Layout and Production - Ron Middlebrook
Tape recorded and engineered by Devin Thomas at
South West Sound in Sierra Madre, California.

Contents

ILLUSTRATION BY BRAD DUTSCH

Dave Celentano

Dave Celentano was fortunate to have a high school buddy named Marty Friedman as a guitar teacher in his early years. After graduating G.I.T. in 1986, Dave went on to author seven guitar books and tapes:
- **The Magic Touch**
- **Flying Fingers**
- **Rock Licks**
- **Speed Metal**
- **The Art of Transcribing**
- **Monster Scales and Modes**
- **Killer Pentatonics**

All Dave's books are published by Centerstream Publishing and can be found in your local music store or ordered from Hal Leonard Publishing.

Also to Dave's credit are a series of Star Lick videos:
- **Randy Rhoads Style**
- **Eric Clapton Style**
- **Guitar Tricks**
- **Scorpions**
- **Aerosmith**
- **Bon Jovi**

Dave's transcribing skills lead him to work with Guitar School Magazine and Hal Leonard Publishing. His transcribing credits include:
- **Alice in Chains 'Face Lift'**
- **Bon Jovi 'New Jersey'**
- **Vixen 'Rev It Up'**
- **Warrant 'D.R.F.S.R.'**
- **Armored Saint 'Symbol of Salvation'**
- **Many columns and songs for Guitar School Magazine.**

Currently, Dave is working on four beginning to intermediate guitar instruction videos for Backstage Pass Videos, teaching at Grayson's Tunetown in Montrose, California and Gard's Music in Glendora, California and performing clinics on the west coast for D'Angelico strings, Wayco straps and W.R.C. (Wayne Charvel) guitars.

Dave's uses D'Angelico strings, Wayco straps and W.R.C. guitars exclusively.

Dave's solo album, "Symphony of Guitars", can be purchased for $7.95 each, plus $2.00 postage (U.S. funds only) from:

Dave Celentano
P.O. Box 1994
Arcadia, California 91077-1994
U.S.A.

Introduction to the Modes

Modes, sometimes referred to as 'church modes', play a major role in an enormous amount of music. Many great musicians including Joe Satriani, Steve Vai, Carlos Santana, Yngwie Malmsteen and Al Di Meola use the modes to their advantage.

Not only will this book show you how to play the modes, it includes theory on how the modes are constructed, how to play any mode in any key, how to play the proper mode over a given chord progression and how to write chord progressions for each of the seven modes.

The cassette tape accompanying this book includes two rhythm tracks (drums, bass, keyboard and rhythm guitar) and a short solo for each mode. After reading through this book carefully, use the rhythm tracks to practice soloing over. This will help you to hear the different 'color sounds' of each mode, because each mode does have it's own individual sound.

Before moving on to the next section you must first understand and memorize the names and order of the modes:

1st	–	Ionian
2nd	–	Dorian
3rd	–	Phrygian
4th	–	Lydian
5th	–	Mixolydian
6th	–	Aeolian
7th	–	Locrian

I'm sorry I can't do anything about the names of these modes. They come from the Greek language and were given to them thousands of years ago.

Explanation of Music Terms and Symbols

1. The modes in this book are charted out on a graph neck diagram like this:

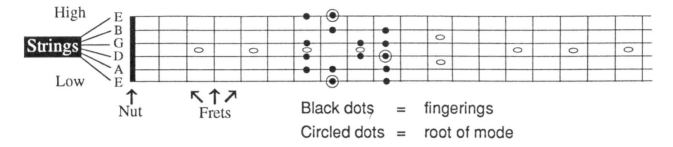

Black dots = fingerings
Circled dots = root of mode

2. The rhythm tracks and lead solos on the accompanying tape are written in 'tablature' at the end of this book:

C major chord

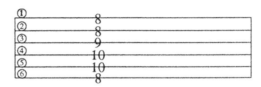

Lines = strings (the bottom line is the low E string on your guitar, the second line from the bottom is the A string, etc.)

Numbers on the lines = frets to place your fingers in.

3. Half step – The distance between any two notes that are one fret apart.

4. Whole step – The distance between any two notes that are two frets apart.

5. Sharp (#) – The sharp symbol indicates the raising of a note by one half step (one fret).

6. Flat (b) – The flat symbol indicates the lowering of a note by one half step (one fret).

7. The 'formula' numbers under all the modes, when described as an alteration, indicate which notes of the Major scale are flatted (b) or sharped (#) to transform it to the desired mode.

How The Seven Modes Are Constructed

Each mode can be thought of or viewed in two different ways:

    1.)   As an <u>inversion</u> of the Major scale.

    2.)   As an <u>alteration</u> of the Major scale.

On the following pages I'm going to explain the seven modes using both ways.

For explaining the modes I'm going to use 'C' as the root note for each mode. This will help make their relationship more visible.

C IONIAN

Ionian   –   Ionian is the first mode, so it begins on the first note of the Major scale. In-other-words the Ionian is just the Major scale.

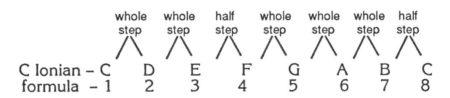

Here's all five finger patterns for C Ionian:

PATTERN 1

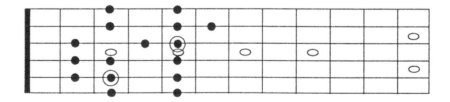

PATTERN 2

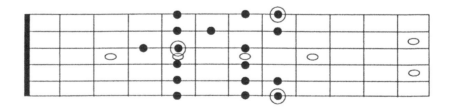

PATTERN 3

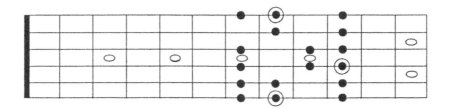

PATTERN 4

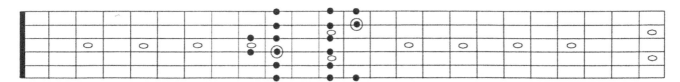

PATTERN 5

C Ionian covering
the entire fretboard

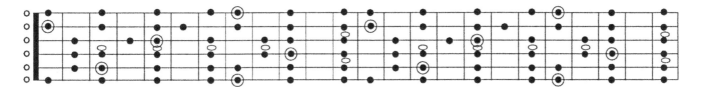

note: The circled notes represent the root note of each mode.
The root of C Ionian is "C". The root of C Dorian is 'C'.

C DORIAN

Dorian – Dorian is the second mode, so it begins on the second note of the Major scale.

    1.) As an inversion, C Dorian is the second mode of B$\flat$ Major:

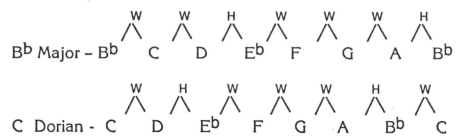

Bb Major – Bb   C   D   Eb   F   G   A   Bb

C Dorian - C   D   Eb   F   G   A   Bb   C

    2.) As an alternation:

C Major –	C	D	E	F	G	A	B	C
formula –	1	2	3	4	5	6	7	8

C Dorian –	C	D	Eb	F	G	A	Bb	C
formula –	1	2	b3	4	5	6	b7	8

By flatting the 3rd and 7th notes of any Major scale by a half step, you have the Dorian mode.

Here's all five finger patterns for C Dorian:

PATTERN 1

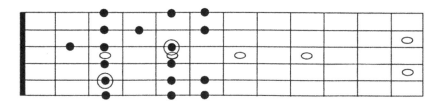

PATTERN 2

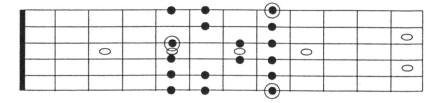

PATTERN 3

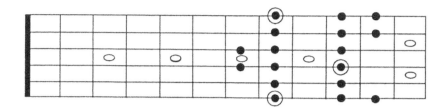

PATTERN 4

PATTERN 5

C Dorian covering
the entire fretboard

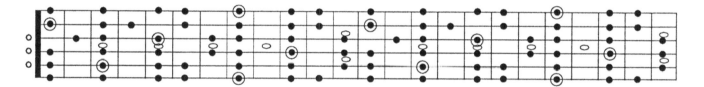

9

C PHRYGIAN

Phrygian – Phrygian is the third mode, so it begins on the third note of the Major scale.

1.) As an inversion, C Phrygian is the third mode of A♭ Major:

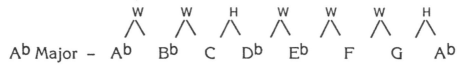

		W		W		H		W		W		W		H	
A♭ Major –	A♭		B♭		C		D♭		E♭		F		G		A♭

		H		W		W		W		H		W		W	
C Phrygian –	C		D♭		E♭		F		G		A♭		B♭		C

2.) As an alternation:

		W		W		H		W		W		W		H	
C Major –	C		D		E		F		G		A		B		C
formula –	1		2		3		4		5		6		7		8

		H		W		W		W		H		W		W	
C Phrygian –	C		D♭		E♭		F		G		A♭		B♭		C
	1		♭2		♭3		4		5		♭6		♭7		8

By flatting the 2nd, 3rd, 6th and 7th notes of any Major scale by a half step, you have the Phrygian mode.

Here's all five finger patterns for C Phrygian:

PATTERN 1

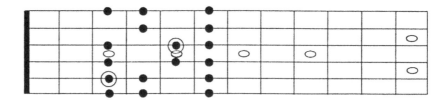

PATTERN 2

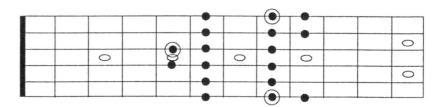

PATTERN 3

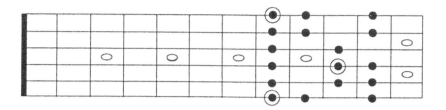

PATTERN 4

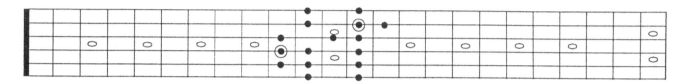

PATTERN 5

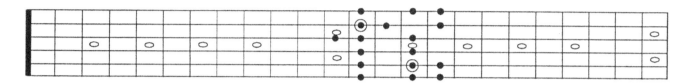

C Phrygian covering
the entire fretboard

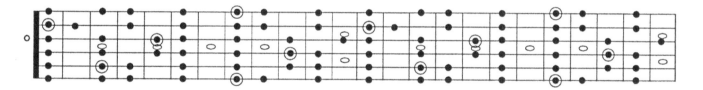

C LYDIAN

Lydian – Lydian is the fourth mode, so it begins on the fourth note of the Major scale.

1.) As an inversion, C Lydian is the fourth mode of G Major:

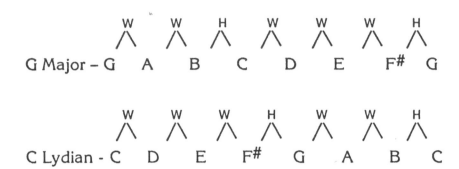

2.) As an alternation:

By sharping the 4th note of any Major scale by a half step, you have the Lydian mode.

Here's all five finger patterns for C Lydian:

PATTERN 1

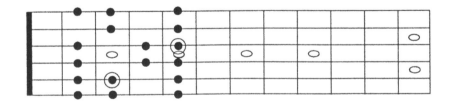

PATTERN 2

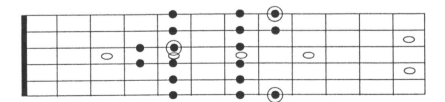

PATTERN 3

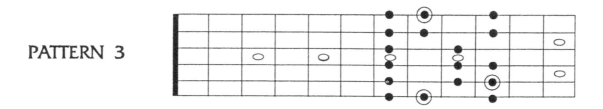

PATTERN 4

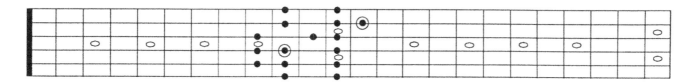

PATTERN 5

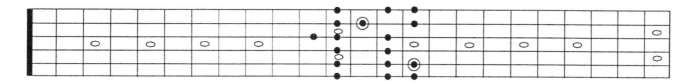

C Lydian covering
the entire fretboard

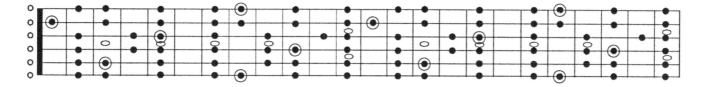

13

C MIXOLYDIAN

Mixolydian – Mixolydian is the fifth mode, so it begins on the fifth note of the Major scale.

1.) As an inversion; C Mixolydian is the fifth mode of F Major:

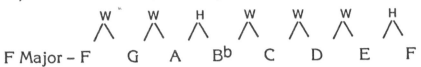

F Major – F G A Bb C D E F

C Mixolydian - C D E F G A Bb C

2.) As an alternation:

C Major – C D E F G A B C
formula – 1 2 3 4 5 6 7 8

C Mixolydian - C D E F G A Bb C
formula – 1 2 3 4 5 6 b7 8

By flatting the 7th note of any Major scale by a half step, you have the Mixolydian mode.

Here's all five patterns for C Mixolydian:

PATTERN 1

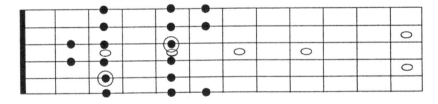

PATTERN 2

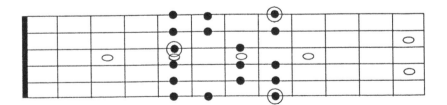

PATTERN 3

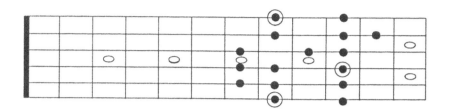

PATTERN 4

PATTERN 5

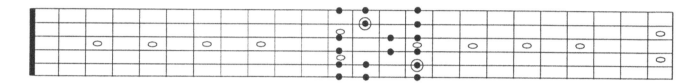

C Mixolydian covering the entire fretboard

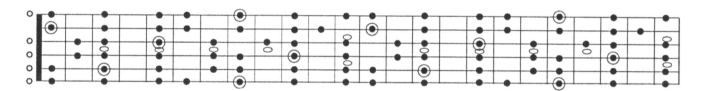

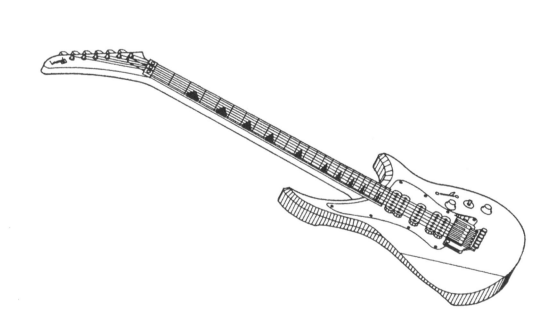

15

Aeolian – Aeolian is the sixth mode, so it begins on the sixth note of the Major scale.

1.) As an inversion, C Aeolian is the sixth mode of E♭ Major:

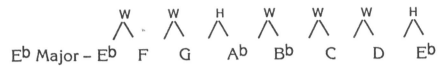

	W	W	H	W	W	W	H

E♭ Major – E♭   F   G   A♭   B♭   C   D   E♭

	W	H	W	W	H	W	W

C Aeolian - C   D   E♭   F   G   A♭   B♭   C

2.) As an alternation:

	W	W	H	W	W	W	H

C Major – C   D   E   F   G   A   B   C

formula – 1   2   3   4   5   6   7   8

	W	H	W	W	H	W	W

C Aeolian – C   D   E♭   F   G   A♭   B♭   C

formula – 1   2   ♭3   4   5   ♭6   ♭7   8

By flatting the 3rd, 6th and 7th notes of any Major scale, you have the Aeolian mode.

Here's all five finger patterns for C Aeolian:

PATTERN 1

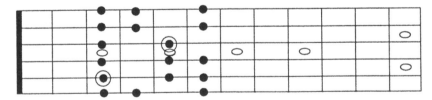

PATTERN 2

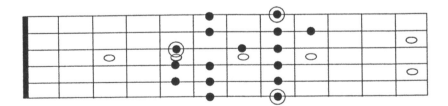

PATTERN 3

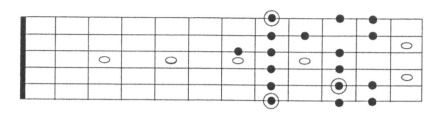

PATTERN 4

PATTERN 5

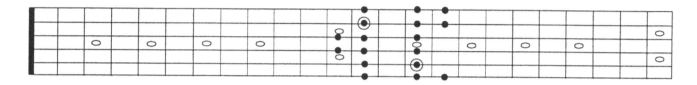

C Aeolian covering the entire fretboard

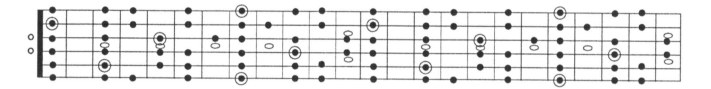

17

C LOCRIAN

Locrian – Locrian is the seventh mode, so it begins on the seventh note of the Major scale.

    1.) As an inversion, C Locrian is the seventh mode of D♭ Major:

$$\overset{W}{\wedge}\quad\overset{W}{\wedge}\quad\overset{H}{\wedge}\quad\overset{W}{\wedge}\quad\overset{W}{\wedge}\quad\overset{W}{\wedge}\quad\overset{H}{\wedge}$$

D♭ Major – D♭   E♭   F   G♭   A♭   B♭   C   D♭

$$\overset{H}{\wedge}\quad\overset{W}{\wedge}\quad\overset{W}{\wedge}\quad\overset{H}{\wedge}\quad\overset{W}{\wedge}\quad\overset{W}{\wedge}\quad\overset{W}{\wedge}$$

C Locrian – C   D♭   E♭   F   G♭   A♭   B♭   C

    2.) As an alteration:

$$\overset{W}{\wedge}\quad\overset{W}{\wedge}\quad\overset{H}{\wedge}\quad\overset{W}{\wedge}\quad\overset{W}{\wedge}\quad\overset{W}{\wedge}\quad\overset{H}{\wedge}$$

C Major – C   D   E   F   G   A   B   C

formula – 1   2   3   4   5   6   7   8

$$\overset{H}{\wedge}\quad\overset{W}{\wedge}\quad\overset{W}{\wedge}\quad\overset{H}{\wedge}\quad\overset{W}{\wedge}\quad\overset{W}{\wedge}\quad\overset{W}{\wedge}$$

C Locrian – C   D♭   E♭   F   G♭   A♭   B♭   C

formula – 1   ♭2   ♭3   4   ♭5   ♭6   ♭7   8

Here's all five finger patterns for C Locrian:

PATTERN 1

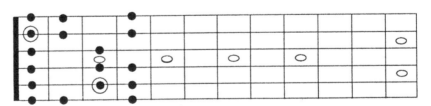

PATTERN 2

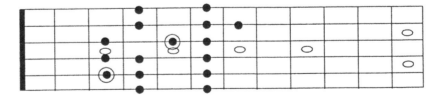

PATTERN 3

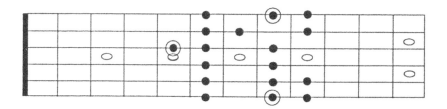

PATTERN 4

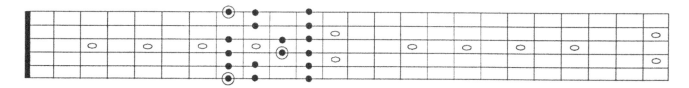

PATTERN 5

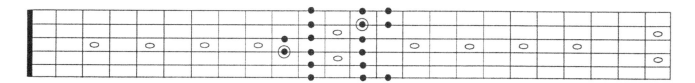

C Locrian covering
the entire fretboard

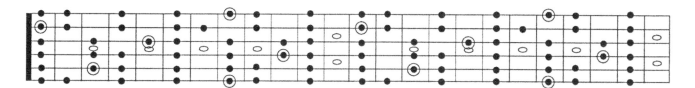

Notice that all seven modes use the same five finger patterns. The only difference is which note functions as the root. So actually playing the modes is the easy part, the hard part is understanding how to apply them and know when to use each particular mode. The next section will explain this.

Modal Chord Progressions

Now that you can play all seven modes, you should learn how to play them properly over the right chord progression.

First, you must understand which chords go with each key or Major scale. In the key of C Major, for instance, the notes are C, D, E, F, G, A, B, C. Each of these notes has chord built from it, so in the key of C Major there is a C chord, D chord, E chord, F chord, etc.

It isn't enough just knowing that a chord is built from each note of the Major scale. You must also understand which ones are major chords and which are minor chords.

Example – Chords in the key of C Major:

I	II	III	IV	V	VI	VII
C major,	D minor,	E minor,	F major,	G major,	A minor,	B diminished

The Roman number over each chord represents the scale degree of the Major scale that the corresponding chords are built from.

The seven chords of every Major scale will <u>always</u> be in this order:

I	II	III	IV	V	VI	VII
major	minor	minor	major	major	minor	diminished

Memorize the order of these chords

Seven Chords of Every Major Scale

Below is a chart of every Major scale along with it's seven corresponding chords:

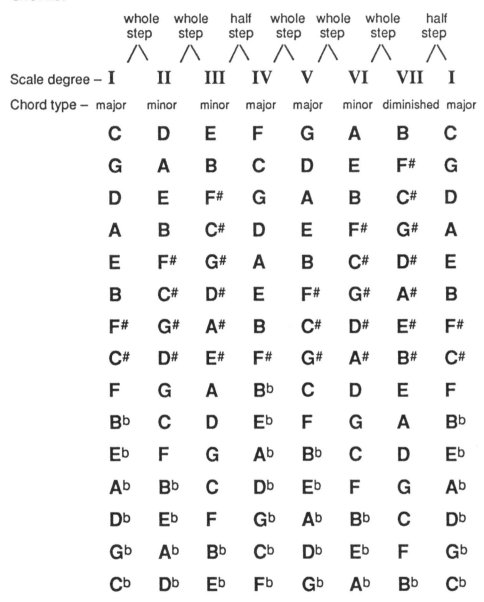

	whole step	whole step	half step	whole step	whole step	whole step	half step	
Scale degree – I	II	III	IV	V	VI	VII	I	
Chord type – major	minor	minor	major	major	minor	diminished	major	
C	D	E	F	G	A	B	C
G	A	B	C	D	E	F#	G
D	E	F#	G	A	B	C#	D
A	B	C#	D	E	F#	G#	A
E	F#	G#	A	B	C#	D#	E
B	C#	D#	E	F#	G#	A#	B
F#	G#	A#	B	C#	D#	E#	F#
C#	D#	E#	F#	G#	A#	B#	C#
F	G	A	Bb	C	D	E	F
Bb	C	D	Eb	F	G	A	Bb
Eb	F	G	Ab	Bb	C	D	Eb
Ab	Bb	C	Db	Eb	F	G	Ab
Db	Eb	F	Gb	Ab	Bb	C	Db
Gb	Ab	Bb	Cb	Db	Eb	F	Gb
Cb	Db	Eb	Fb	Gb	Ab	Bb	Cb

Remember, the first note of every Major scale is also the key or root of the Major scale. This chart is a good reference to help you quickly figure out all the chords of any given key.

Example – Say if you need to know what chords are in the key of B Major. Look down the first column until you find the 'B' note. Now look across the row of B major. The chords you should have found are:

B major, **C#** minor, **D#** minor, **E** major, **F#** major, **G#** minor, **A#** diminished and **B** major

21

If you don't know how to play all the chords on the chart, pick up a chord book at your local music store. A good chord book should have diagrams of all these chords.

What does all of this have to do with the modes? Well, I'm going to use the chords of the Major scale to show you how to write "modal chords progressions" for you to improvise over.

Before we go on let me point out that for all the "modal chord progressions" I'm going to show them to you with 'C' as the root of each mode. This will correspond with the modes I diagramed and explained in the previous chapter "How the Modes Are Constructed".

The first mode is Ionian (remember that Ionian is just the Major scale). We'll use C Ionian. Look at the chords of C Major on the chord chart:

C major, D minor, E minor, F major, G major, A minor, and B diminished

Now experiment by playing different combinations of those chords. To emphasize the Ionian sound you should start the chord progression on the C major chord (I chord).

$$\|\colon \text{C major} \mid \text{A minor} \mid \text{F major} \mid \text{G major} \colon\|$$

Another thing I'd like to point out is that on some of these modal chord progressions I'm going to use the root note of the mode as the bass note for all the chords in the progression.

$$\|\colon \text{C maj.} \mid \underset{\text{C}}{\overset{\text{G maj.}}{}} \mid \underset{\text{C}}{\overset{\text{F maj.}}{}} \mid \text{C} \colon\|$$

The 'C' under the 'G' and 'F' chords means you play a G major chord and use 'C' as the bass (lowest) note. Do the same thing for the F major chord. This concept helps to bring out the color of the mode.

On the cassette tape accompanying this book I've included two different rhythm tracks and solos for each mode. We'll go in order of the modes, so the first two exercises will be rhythms using the Ionian mode. Use the five finger patterns for C Ionian discussed earlier in this book to solo over these rhythms.

C Ionian

Rhythm

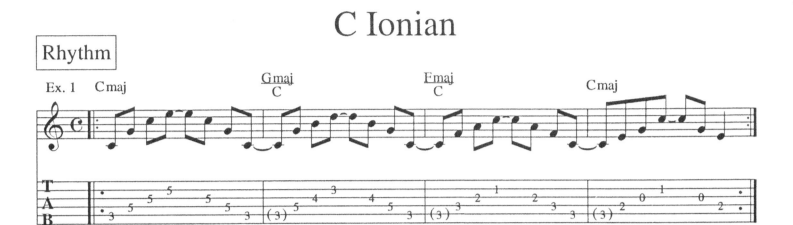

Lead Solo

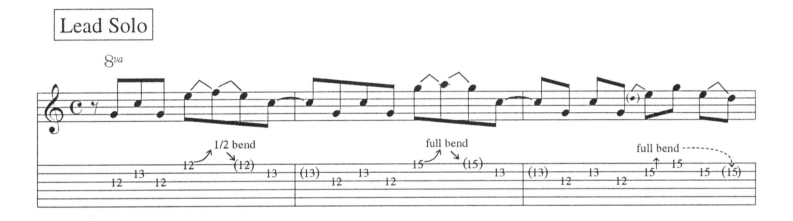

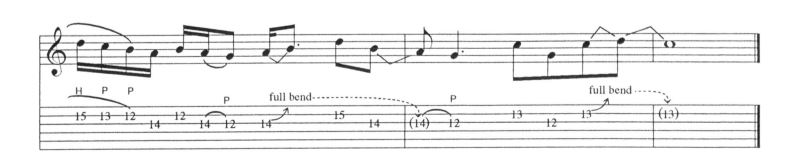

C Ionian

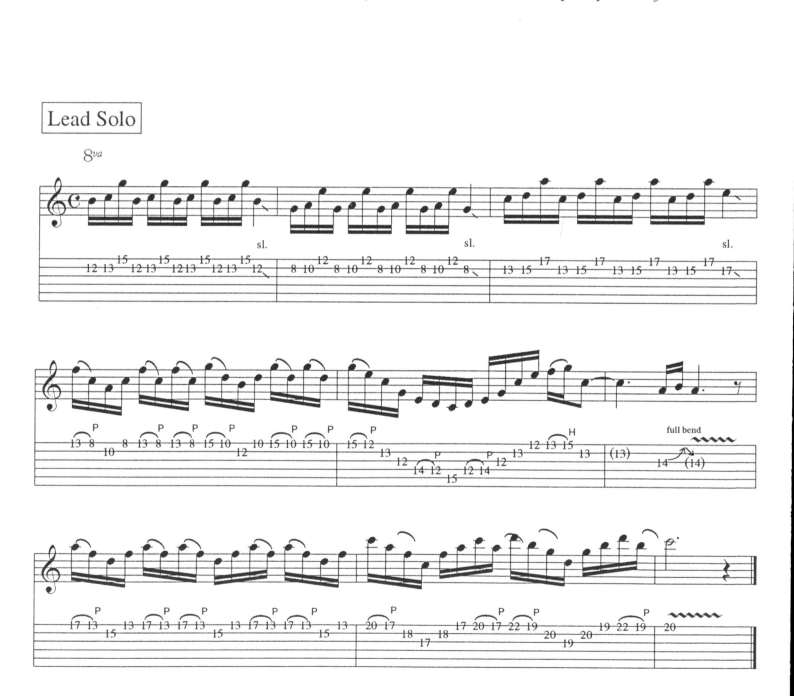

The second mode is Dorian. We'll use C Dorian, which is derived from the second note in B♭ Major. Look at the B♭ Major key on the chord chart. These will be the chords you'll use to write a modal chord progression for C Dorian:

B♭ major, C minor, D minor, E♭ major, F major, G minor, A diminished

Use the five finger patterns for C Dorian to improvise over exercises 3 and 4.
Eddie Van Halen and Carlos Santana are often associated with this soulful sounding mode.

C Dorian

C Dorian

Rhythm

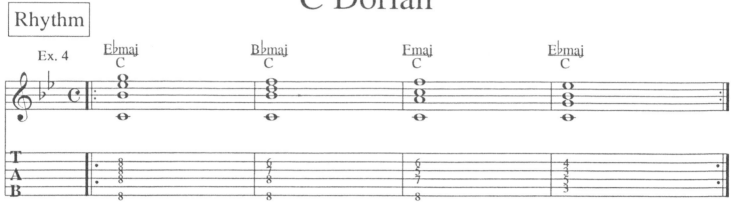

Lead Solo

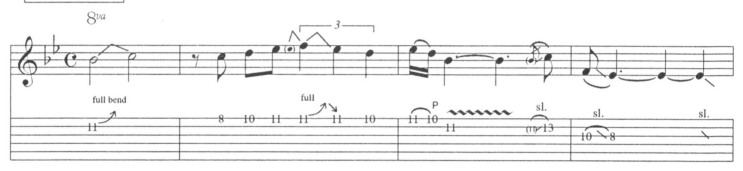

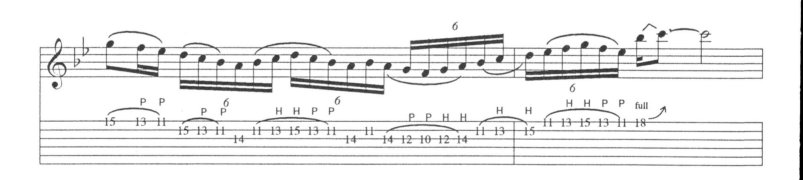

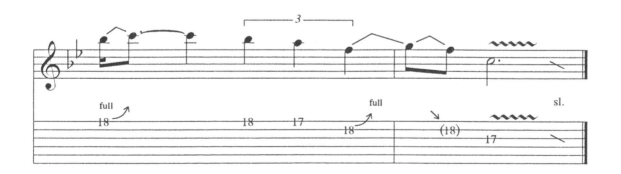

26

The third mode is Phrygian. We'll use C Phrygian, which is derived from the third note in A♭ Major. Here's the chords you'll use to write a modal chord progression for C Phrygian:

A♭ major, B♭ minor, C minor, D♭ major, E♭ major, F minor, G diminished
Use the five finger pattern for C Phrygian to improvise over exercises 5 and 6.
Yngwie Malmsteen and Al Di Meola love using this eerie sounding mode.

C Phrygian

Rhythm

Lead Solo

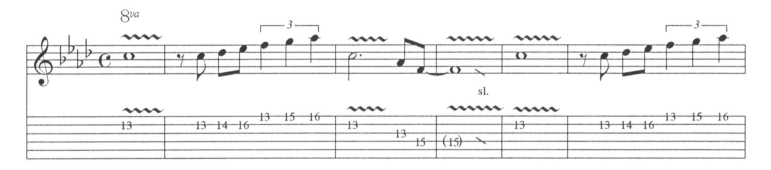

27

C Phrygian

Lead Solo

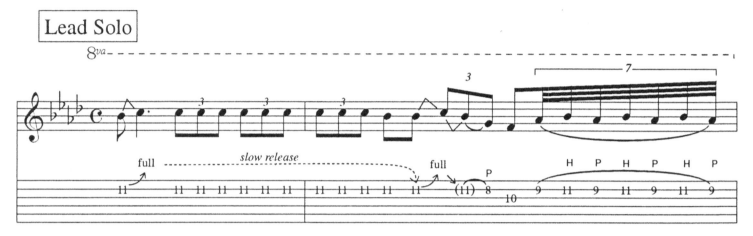

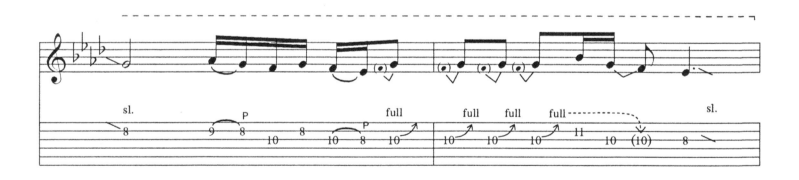

28

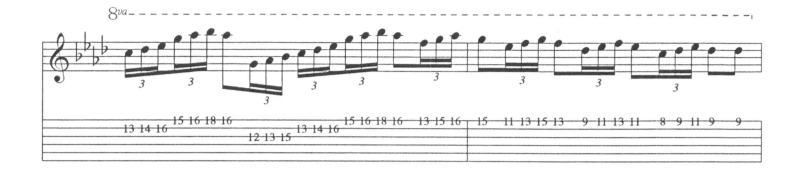

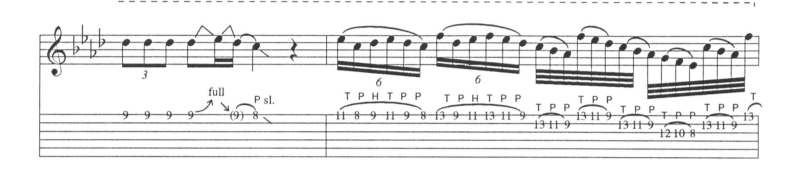

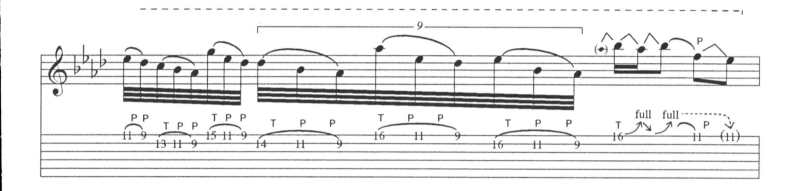

The fourth mode is Lydian. We'll use C Lydian, which is derived from the fourth note in G Major. Here's the chords you'll use to write a modal chord progression for C Lydian:

G major, A minor, B minor, C major, D major, E minor, F# diminished

Use the five finger patterns for C Lydian to improvise over exercises 7 and 8.
Although this mode is used often in contemporary jazz, it can also be heard in the music of Joe Satriani and Steve Vai.

C Lydian

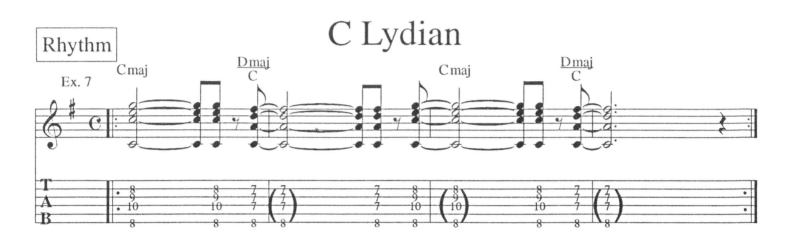

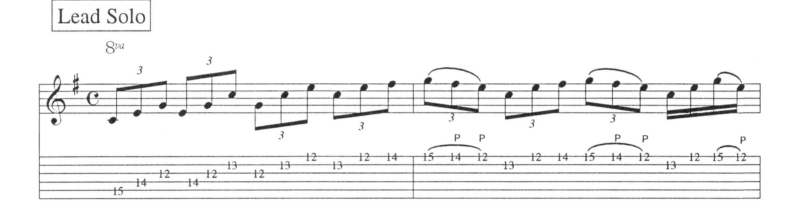

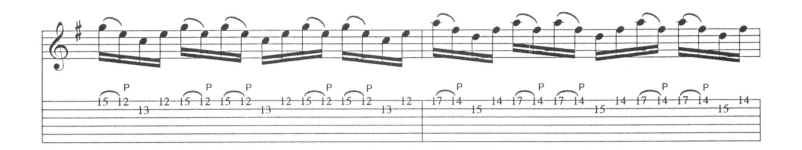

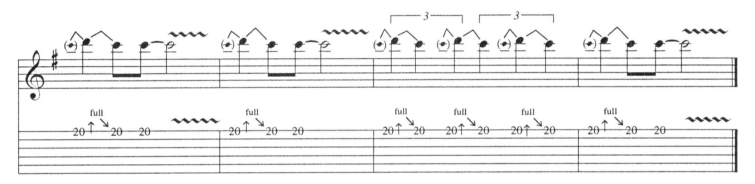

Dave Celentano

C Lydian

Rhythm

Lead Solo

32

The fifth mode is Mixolydian. We'll use C Mixolydian, which is derived from the fifth note in F Major. Here's the chords you'll use to write a modal chord progression for C Mixolydian:

F major, G minor, A minor, B♭ major, C major, D minor, E diminished

Use the five finger patterns for C Mixolydian to improvise over exercises 9 and 10. This bluesy sounding mode is a characteristic trait in the improvising work of many rock guitarists including Micheal Schenker and Slash of Guns and Roses.

C Mixolydian

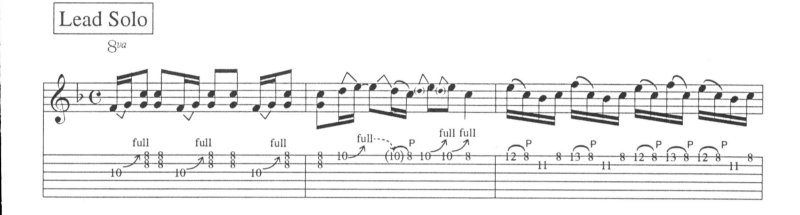

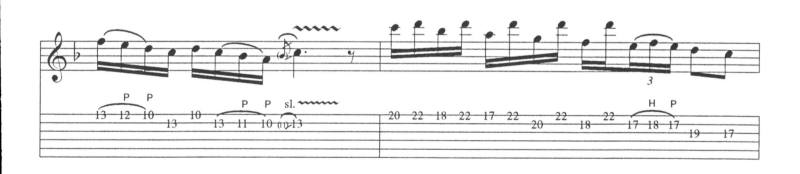

33

C Mixolydian

The sixth mode is Aeolian. We'll use C Aeolian, which is derived from the sixth note in
E♭ Major. Here's the chords you'll use to write a modal chord progression for C Aeolian:

E♭ major, F minor, G minor, A♭ major, B♭ major, C minor, D diminished

Use the five finger patterns for C Aeolian to improvise over exercises 11 and 12.
This dark sounding mode is one of the most frequently used scales in heavy metal. Randy
Rhoads used it often.

C Aeolian

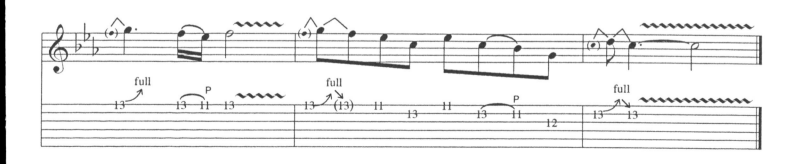

35

C Aeolian

The seventh mode is Locrian. We'll use C Locrian, which is derived from the seventh note of D♭ Major. Here's the chords you'll use to write a modal chord progression for C Locrian:

D♭ major, E♭ minor, F minor, G♭major , A♭ major, B♭ minor, C diminished
Use the five finger patterns for C Locrian to improvise over exercises 13 and 14.
Because of the 'outside' sound of this mode, it is primarily used in jazz music.

C Locrian

37

C Locrian

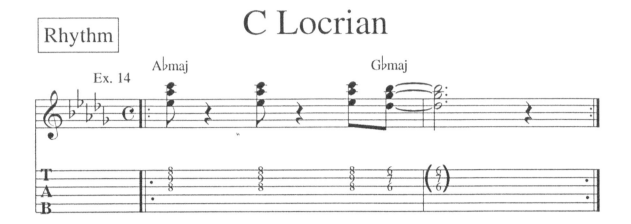

Lead Solo

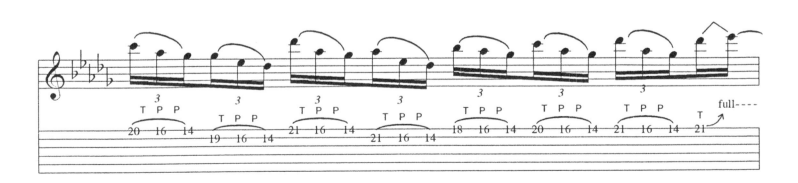

38

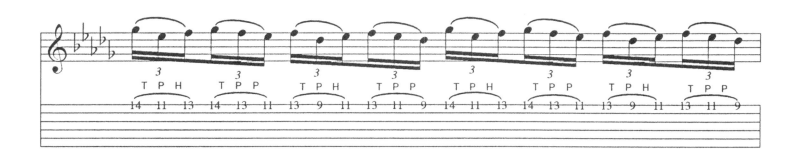

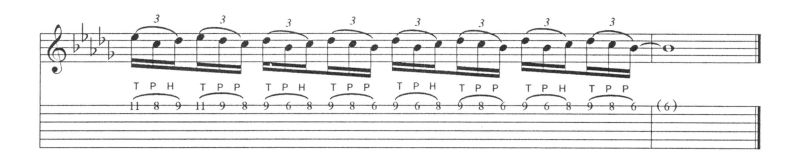

All the information and concepts I've presented to you on the seven modes and modal chords progressions can and should be applied to all keys. Remember that each mode can start on any note. Say you want to play A Phrygian. Phrygian is the third mode, and 'A' is the third note of F Major (F, G, A, B♭, C, D, E, F), so A Phrygian would read: A, B♭, C, D, E, F, G, A. Now you would go to the five finger patterns for Phrygian *diagramed earlier in this book* and move each one back three frets, so that all the circled root notes are now on A's.

When writing a modal chord progression for A Phrygian you would go to the chart (page 21) "Seven Chords of Every Major Scale" *diagramed earlier in this book* and look down the first column at the chords of F Major. These chords should read:

F major, G minor, A minor, B♭ major, C major, D minor, E diminished
Use these chords to write a modal chord progression for A Phrygian.

Now you should have a clearer understanding of how to use the modes. Soloing over the rhythm tracks on the accompanying cassette will help you to hear the true characteristic sounds of each mode. *Gook Luck!*

If you have any questions, comments or would like free information on all Dave's books and tapes, write to:

Flying Fingers Productions
P.O. Box 1994
Arcadia, California 91077-1994
U.S.A.